WASHOE COUNTY LIBRARY
3 1235 01144 0414

D0536090

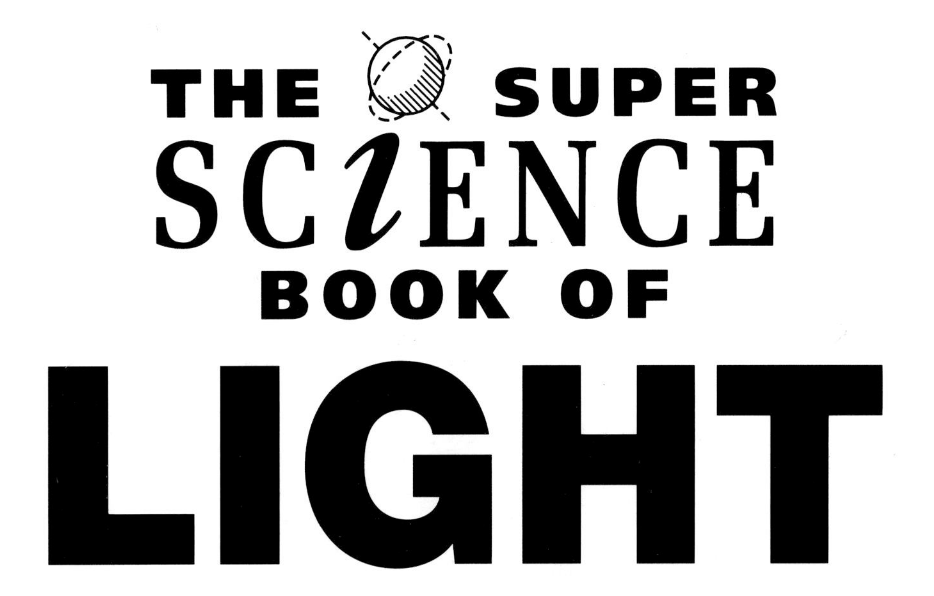

Graham Peacock and Terry Hudson

Lights Out!

My little sister hates "Lights Out," she throws a fit—boy can she shout!
All red-faced she stamps and screams, "But Mom, I have such nasty dreams!"
Me, I'm different. I like night. Through my curtains stars shine bright.
And as the moon sails through the clouds, a galleon in ghostly shrouds,
I see patterns in the sky, a picture book way up on high,
Catch a falling star or two. What is light and dark to you?

My little sister wakes with the sun, fresh as a daisy, calls our Mom.
"Can I go outside and play? What we gonna do today?"
Me, I'm not my best at dawn, all that I can do is yawn,
Snuggle deeper down the covers (wish that she had been a brother).

My little sister, she likes light but I'm a creature of the night!

by Catherine Baxter

Illustrations by Frances Lloyd

Thomson Learning
New York

Titles in the Super Science series

The Environment
Light
Materials
Our Bodies
Time
Weather

First published in the
United States in 1993 by
Thomson Learning
115 Fifth Avenue
New York, NY 10003

First published in 1993 by
Wayland (Publishers) Ltd.

Cataloging-in-Publication Data applied for

ISBN: 1-56847-022-3
Printed in Italy

Series Editor: Cally Chambers
Designer: Loraine Hayes Design

Picture acknowledgments

Illustrations by Frances Lloyd.
Cover illustration by Martin Gordon.

Photographs by permission of: Ancient Art and Architecture Collection 7; Biophotos 24, 25 bottom; Jeff Greenburg 13; Science Photo Library 5 (NASA), 6 (NASA), 10 (Gordon Garrad), 12 bottom (JL Charmet), 17 bottom (David Parker), 19 (Western Ophthalmic Hospital), 21 top (Keith Kent), 21 bottom (Adam Hart-Davis), 23 (Françoise Sauze), 27 top (Chris Bjornberg), 28 (Philippe Plailly), 29 bottom (BSIP Bajande); Zefa 9, 12 top, 15, 16, 17 top, 20, 25, 29 top.

CONTENTS

STARLIGHT

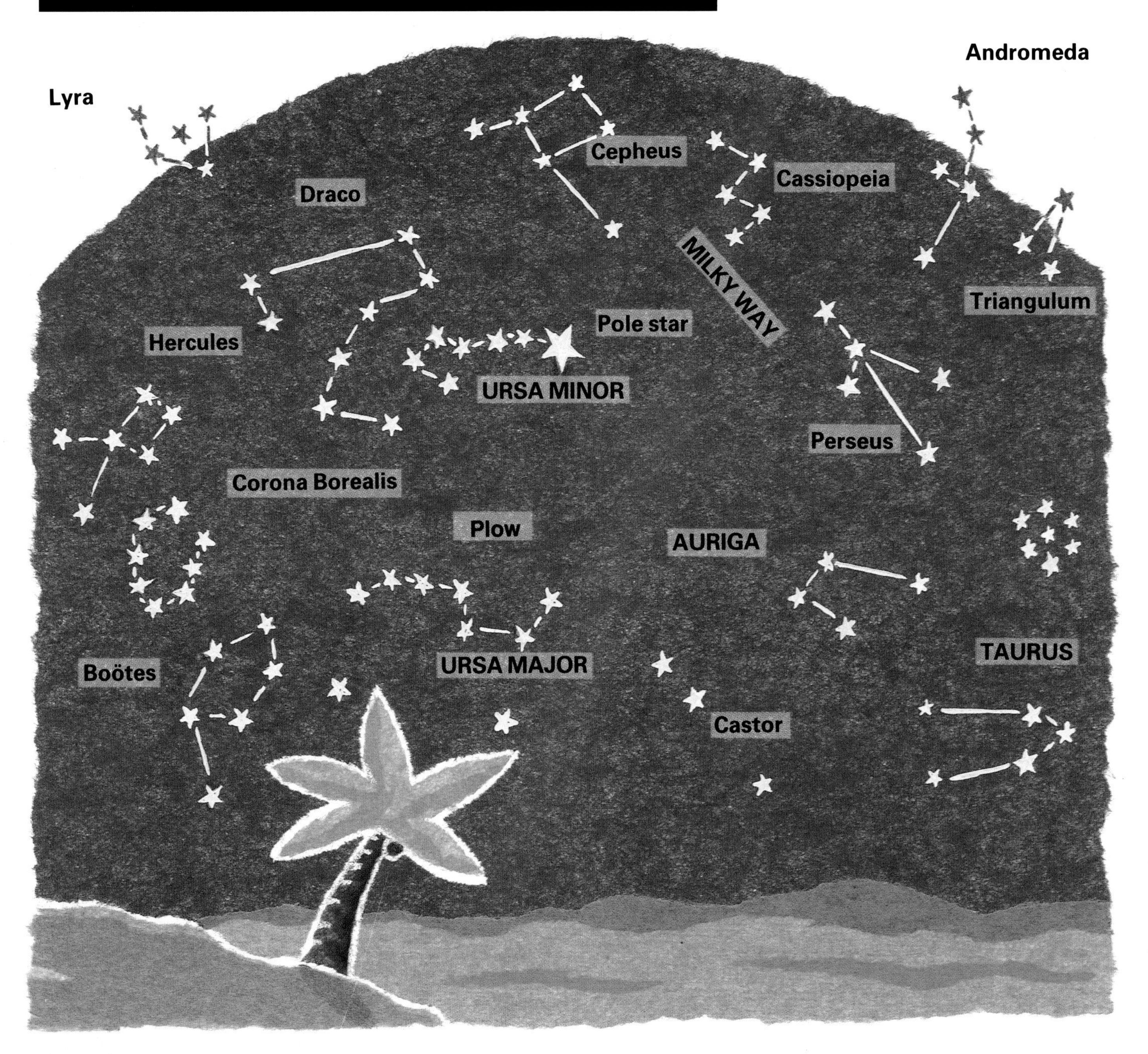

▲When you look up on a dark, cloudless night the whole sky seems to be filled with the light of stars. In ancient times, people thought they could see patterns or shapes in the stars—a bit like a giant connect-the-dots. They gave many of the shapes names. They called one the Plow because they thought they could see the shape of a plow outlined by the stars. The ancient Greeks invented stories about these groups of stars or constellations. They called one constellation Andromeda, after a beautiful girl in a story who was rescued from a sea monster. Next time it is a clear, cloudless night, take a look yourself! See if you can make out any shapes in the stars.

The amount of starlight we receive here on Earth is very small because the stars are so far away. The nearest star—apart from the sun, which is a star—is called Alpha Centauri. It is 25 trillion miles away. Even though light travels incredibly fast, the light from Alpha Centauri takes more than four years to reach Earth. The light from distant stars takes even longer.

Astronomers are scientists who study the stars. Today the glow from the lights in cities makes it difficult to see the stars clearly. So astronomers usually build their telescopes high up on mountains in remote places where the light from cities doesn't interfere. If you want the best view of the stars, go as far into the countryside as you can so that you can see the sky clearly.

▲ Sailors steered their ships by using the stars as a giant map.

▲ Sometimes, telescopes are even sent into space. In space, they get away from the dust particles in Earth's atmosphere that stop some of the dimmest starlight from reaching the earth. This is a photograph of the Hubble telescope being taken out into space.

SUNLIGHT

The sun is the star ▶ nearest Earth. It provides light and heat for Earth. This image of the sun was recorded by a special instrument on board the Skylab space station. Color has been added to it.

The sun is at its hottest at its center. Here, temperatures are as high as 25 million degrees Fahrenheit (°F). The outer parts of the sun are much cooler at only 11,000°F—although this is still hot enough to melt steel easily! Huge flames of glowing gas leap from the surface of the sun.

◀ The sun is about 93 million miles from Earth. It takes about eight minutes for its light to reach us. If the jet airliner Concorde could travel in space, and you bought a ticket to the sun, it would take you more than 20 years to get there!

Many ancient peoples realized that the sun was very important to life on Earth. They knew that without it, plants would not grow, and that without plants to eat, animals would die. Because of this, they worshiped the sun as a god.

◀ The most important god for the ancient Egyptians was Ra, the sun god. In fact, the whole Egyptian city of Heliopolis was devoted to worshiping and studying the sun. The ancient peoples of Mexico and Peru were the Aztecs and the Incas. They also worshiped the sun and built magnificent temples. Sometimes they killed people to offer them as gifts to the sun.

WOW!
The sun looks very bright from Earth. But from Pluto–the most distant planet in our solar system–you would find it hard to tell the sun from other stars.

PLANTS AND LIGHT

Green plants are the only living things that can change the energy of the sun's light into food. With the energy of the sun, carbon dioxide in the air, and water, plants can produce much more complicated substances like glucose, a simple type of sugar. This astonishing feat is called photosynthesis. The word photosynthesis is made up from two words: photo, which means "light," and synthesis, which means "to make."

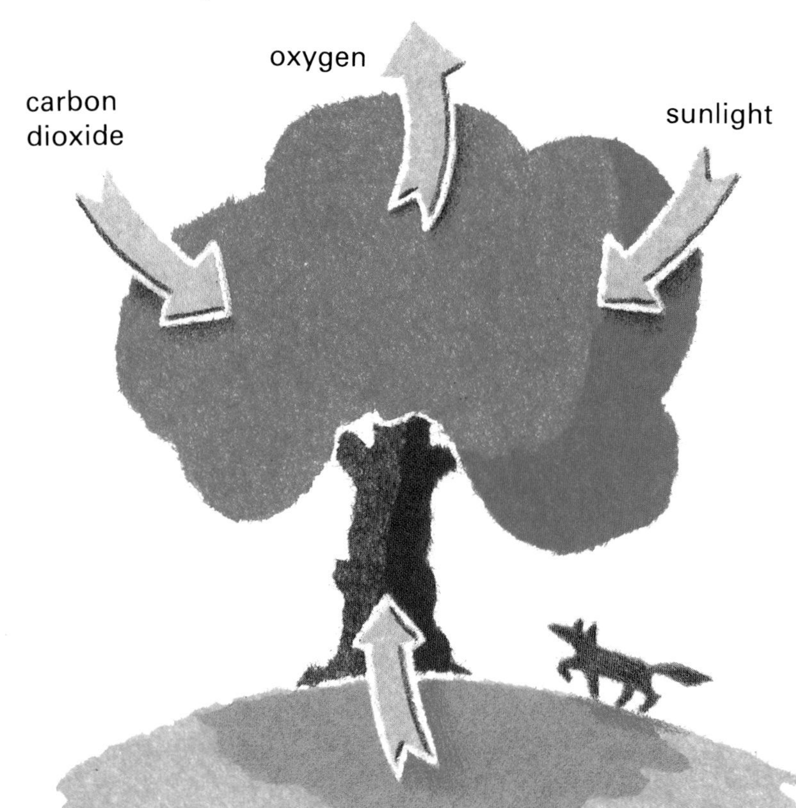

◀ During the day when it is light, plants produce oxygen through photosynthesis. They release the oxygen into the air. During the night, plants break down the food that they have made during the day, and in doing so release some carbon dioxide.

WOW!
Some plants will grow toward light even if they have to break through concrete to get to it. They can even grow through mazes to reach the light.

Plants need to make the best use of sunlight. So as the sun moves across the sky, some plants actually position their leaves to get as much light as possible. Seedlings grow toward the sun and can become quite tall in their search for light.

ENERGY FROM LIGHT

People have invented ways to use the energy from the sun directly. Solar cells are able to change sunlight into electricity. In some very sunny places, like Arizona, solar cells can make enough electricity to supply whole houses. ▶

Another way in which we can make use of sunlight directly is to make a solar furnace. This reflects the sun's light and heat onto a boiler, where water is heated to make steam. This steam can turn turbines and make electricity.

The best solar panels are made so that they turn during the day to get the most sunlight. This is how the leaves of some plants behave. ▼

LIGHTING UP

Hot things, like the sun or a burning piece of wood, produce light. Firelight was present on the earth millions of years before the first people appeared. Natural fires happened then, as they do today. For example, fires would have started when red-hot rocks from volcanic eruptions touched dry grass or during violent storms, such as this, when lightning struck trees. ▶

◀ The first artificial light used by people were made from burning pieces of wood. Sitting in the glow from a camp fire, Stone Age people must have felt safe from attack by wild animals. Wood fires are often dangerous inside rooms or tents, so people developed lamps that burned with a small, bright flame. The first fuel to be used in lamps was probably the fat of animals. The Inuit people of the Arctic used seal or whale blubber in lamps they carved from soft rock.

◀ Miners who dig underground have always needed a good source of light to see by. Today, they use electric lamps powered by batteries, but in early times they had to use candles or oil lamps. This was dangerous, because in some mines a gas called methane built up, which could explode if a bare flame was used. However, in 1815, a scientist called Humphrey Davy invented a safety lamp whose flame changed color if there was methane in the air. It did not set fire to any methane in the air because the lamp's flame was surrounded by a special kind of wire gauze.

◀ We still use candlelight on special occasions. Many people have a cake decorated with burning candles on their birthdays. Jewish people celebrate Hanukkah by burning eight candles to commemorate the rededication of a great temple.

Today, lighthouses use electric lamps to warn ships of dangerous rocks around coastlines. Before electric lamps were invented, people used to build large fires on the cliff tops to warn ships. ▶

WOW!

The brightest light from a lighthouse in Britain is that on Stumble Head, near Fishguard, in Wales. The light is equivalent to six million candles.

ELECTRIC LIGHT

WOW!
The brightest electric light was a searchlight made during World War II. It produced a light equivalent to 2.7 billion candles.

Today we use electric light instead of gas or oil lamps and candles. Electricity can give us much brighter light, and it is less likely to cause a fire. Electricity can be used to make light in two main ways.

▼Fluorescent tubes are partly filled with a special gas. When an electrical current flows through the gas, it gives off tiny particles that hit the phosphor coating of the glass tube, causing it to glow.

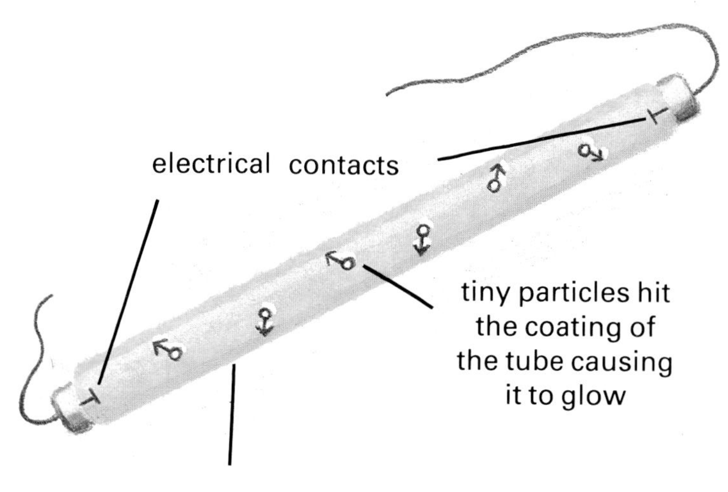

▲Electric bulbs produce light when electricity passes through a very thin piece of wire called a filament. Filament wires slow down the flow of electricity, and in doing so become very hot and give out light. One of the earliest light bulbs was invented in 1879 by American inventor Thomas Edison. ▶

MOVING PICTURES

Your television set makes light in a way similar to a fluorescent tube. In the television tube, tiny particles come from a special gun at the rear of the tube. When the tiny particles hit the phosphor coating on the screen, they cause it to glow. This makes only a single point of light, but by going backward and forward more quickly than your eye can follow, the whole picture is made.

Moving pictures are made by shining a bright light through a piece of colored film. The light shines onto a screen, and from there it is reflected into your eye. Single pictures are projected for such a short time that your eye does not notice when they change, so you get the impression of continuous movement. Have you ever watched an old Charlie Chaplin movie? It looks very jerky. This is because the earliest movies moved very slowly through the projector, and there weren't as many pictures.

Make a "Moving" Picture Book

1 Take a small notebook, or a telephone book, and draw a simple "stick" person at the bottom right-hand corner of the first page. Then continue drawing the same person throughout the book. Each time, your person must be in a slightly different position.

2 Now flip through the book and see the person move!

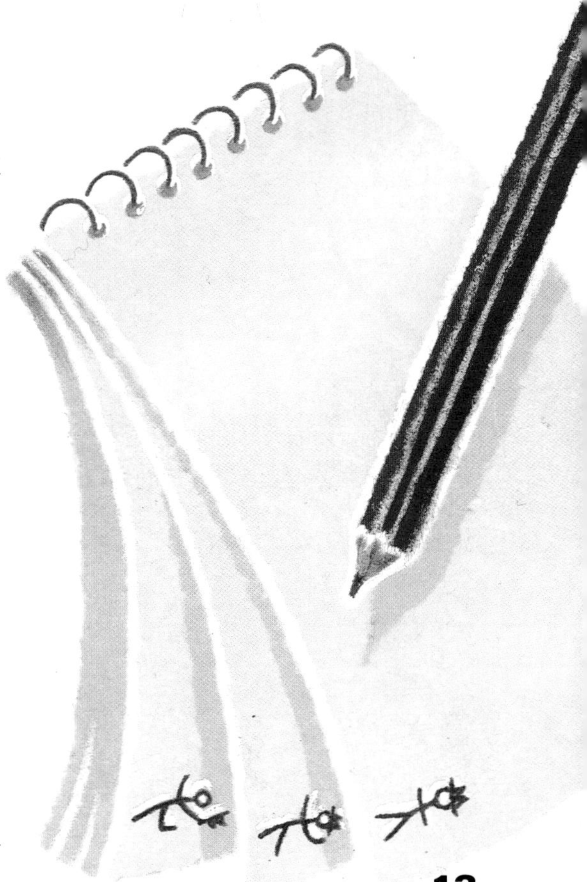

MIRRORS MIRRORS

Light travels in straight lines and bounces off objects that it hits. If the object's surface is rough, then the light bounces off in all different directions. If the surface is smooth and shiny, the light bounces off in one direction and forms a reflection, or image. Polished metal is a good reflector. This is why most glass mirrors are coated on the back with shiny silver. ▶

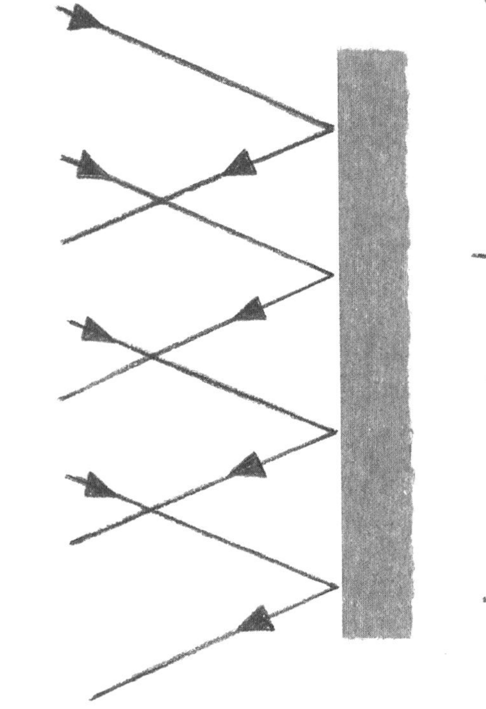

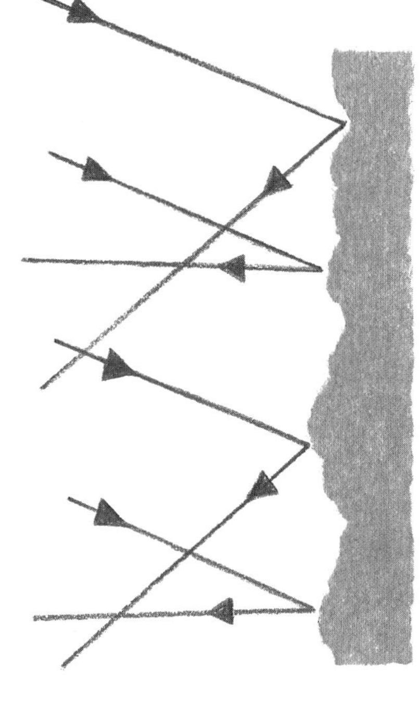

◀ When light hits a mirror at an angle, it bounces off at the same angle. You can see this for yourself by getting a flashlight and sticking a large circle of thick black paper over the end. Make a small hole in the middle of the paper, and shine the flashlight at a mirror in a dark room.

In a mirror, the reflection is always backward—you even see yourself backward. The famous artist and scientist, Leonardo da Vinci, wrote some of his notes in mirror writing to keep people from seeing what he was writing. If you want to read the message below, you will probably have to hold it up to a mirror. ▼

can you read
this message?...

◀ Curved mirrors are very useful. Headlights and flashlights use concave mirrors, which curve inward. They reflect the light in a straight beam instead of letting it spread out in all directions. When you stand close to a concave shaving mirror, your reflection is magnified.

Convex mirrors, which curve outward, are used to give a wide field of view. They are used on car door mirrors to give the driver a wide view behind the car.

Many old stories tell of the power that people thought mirrors had. In the fairy tale, Snow White's stepmother had a mirror that told her who was the most beautiful woman in the world.

◀ In one Greek legend, the hero Perseus used a mirror made from a brightly polished shield to reflect the image of the Gorgon. If Perseus had looked at the Gorgon directly, he would have been turned to stone.

WOW!
An enormous mirror measuring about 33 ft. in diameter is being built for an observatory in the U.S.

LENSES

Light travels through transparent materials almost as if they weren't there. Translucent materials keep some of the light from getting through, and opaque materials completely block light. This explains why we can see through transparent and translucent materials but not through opaque ones. When light travels from one transparent material to another, it usually bends. For example, when light passes from the air into water it is bent. This is why a pencil in a glass of water appears to be crooked. ▶

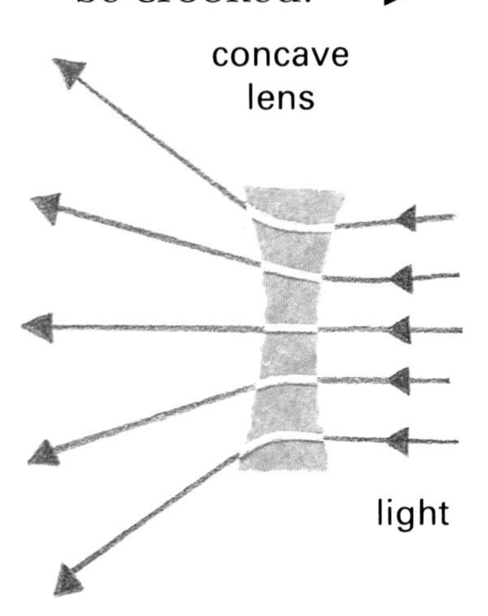

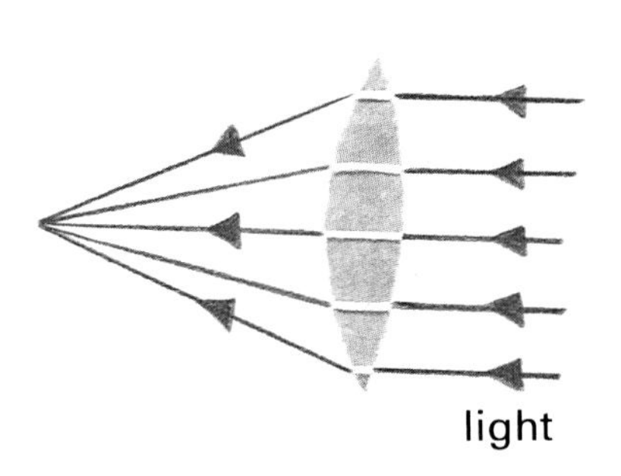

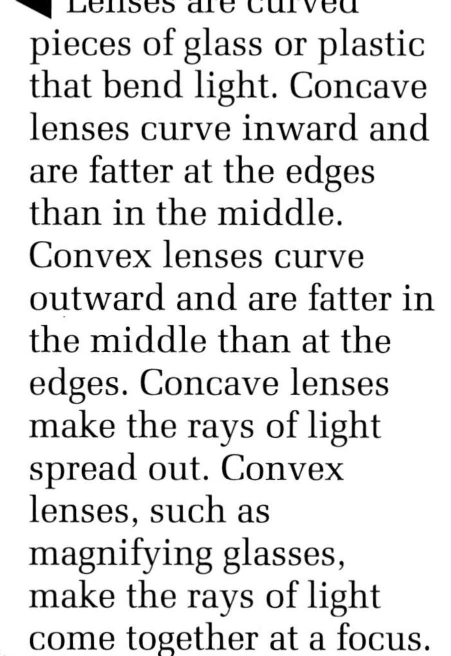
◀ Lenses are curved pieces of glass or plastic that bend light. Concave lenses curve inward and are fatter at the edges than in the middle. Convex lenses curve outward and are fatter in the middle than at the edges. Concave lenses make the rays of light spread out. Convex lenses, such as magnifying glasses, make the rays of light come together at a focus.

Making a Magnifier

You can make a magnifying lens yourself. Simply lay a sheet of thin, clear plastic on a newspaper or book and place a single drop of water on the plastic. What happens to the size of the printed words beneath? ▶

Our eyes have lenses in them that help us to see. However, many people's vision can be improved by glasses, which are extra lenses for the eye. Some lenses are placed on the surface of the eye. These are called contact lenses. ▶

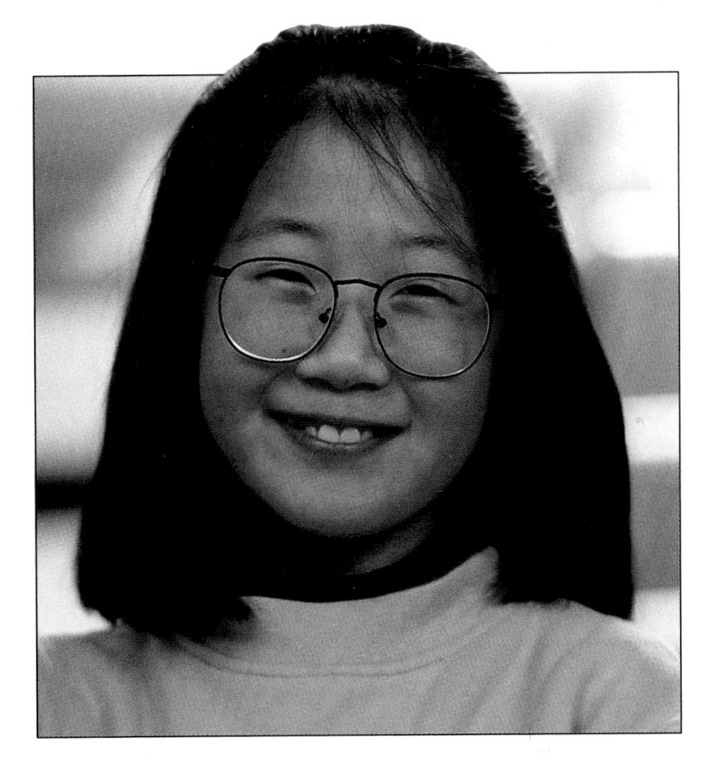

All modern cameras have lenses that focus light. The simplest cameras have a single convex lens. The light passes through the lens and forms an upside-down image on the film. The film is coated with a chemical that changes when light falls on it.

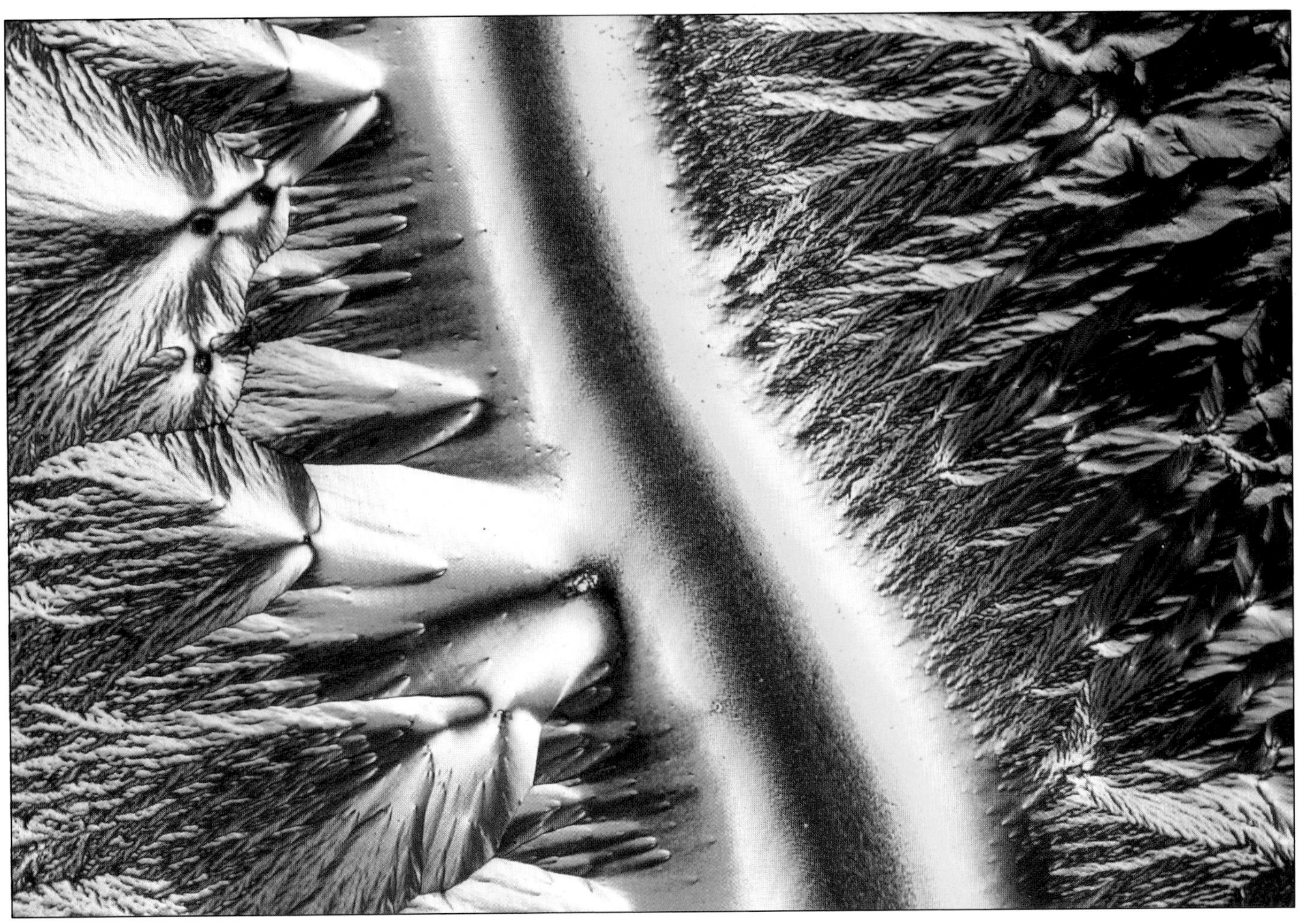

▲ Believe it or not, this is what vitamin C crystals look like through a microscope. Microscopes use lenses to magnify very tiny objects up to 3,000 times their size. This picture has had color added to help you see the shapes.

THE EYE

We see the things around us when the light they give off or reflect enters our eyes. This picture shows a cross section of an eye.

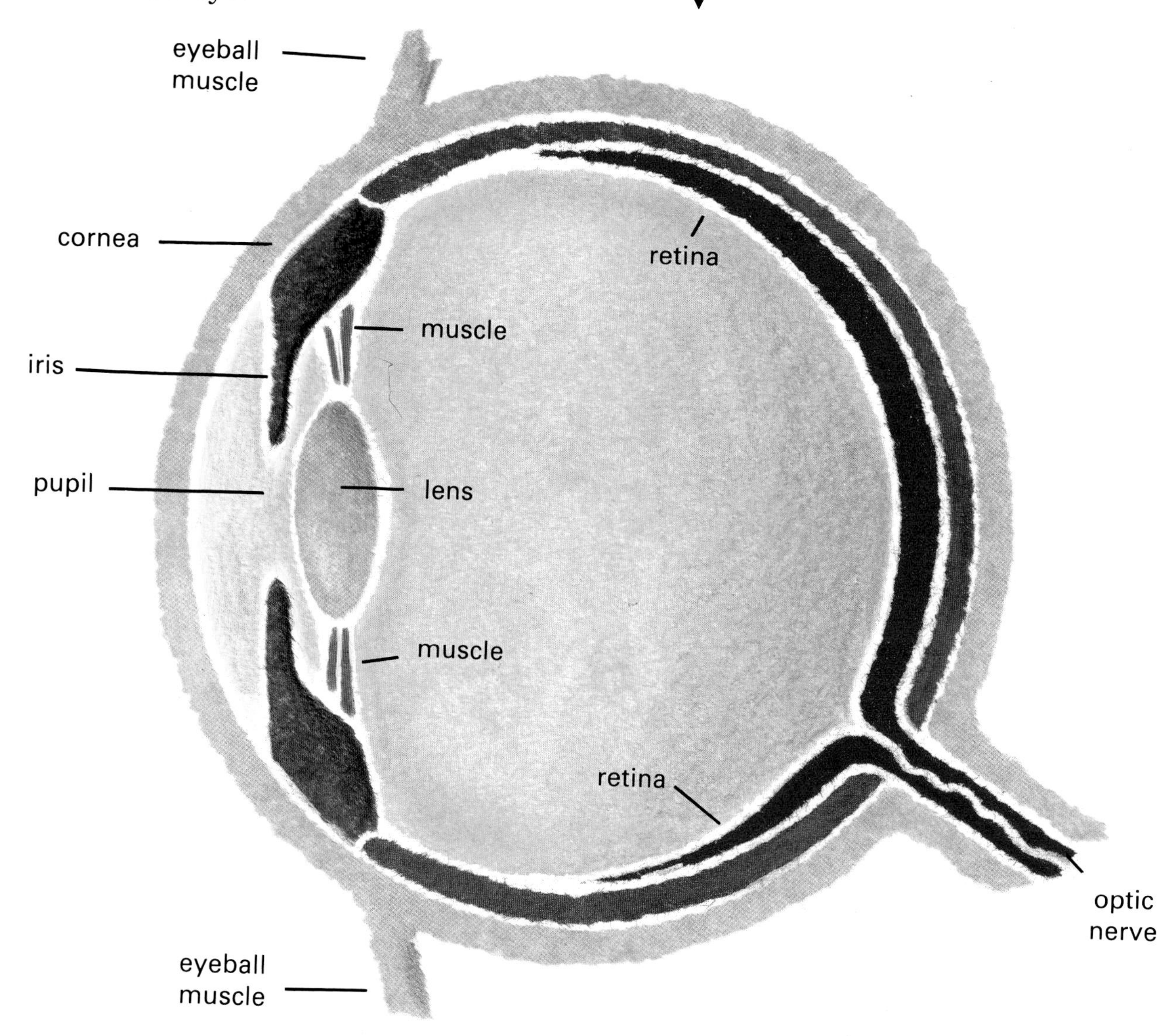

The first layer that light has to go through is the transparent covering of the eye, called the cornea. Next, the light passes through the lens which, along with the cornea, focuses the light onto the retina at the back of the eye. In the retina, the light is turned into electrical signals. These signals are sent along the optic nerve straight to the brain, which makes sense of them and tells you what you are looking at.

The black dot in the middle of each of your eyes is called a pupil. The pupil is the hole through which light enters the eye. The size of this hole is controlled by a muscle called the iris. The iris makes the hole large when the light is dim and closes up the pupil when there is bright light. ▶

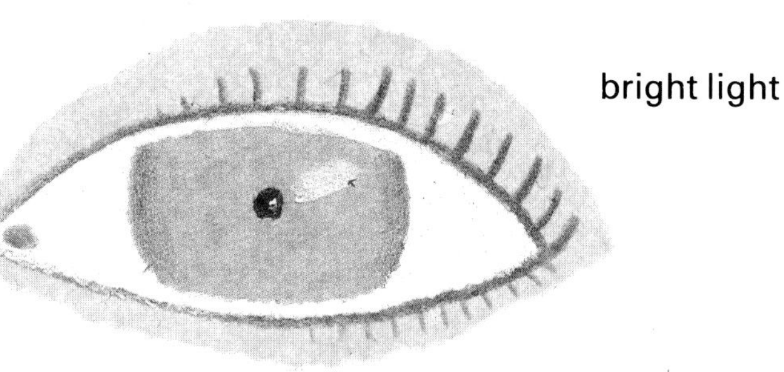

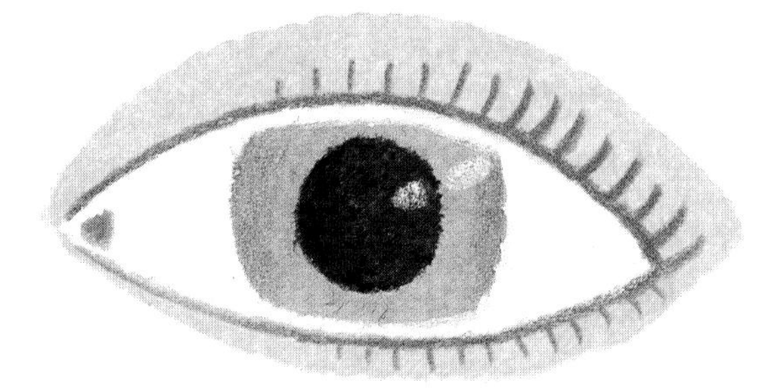

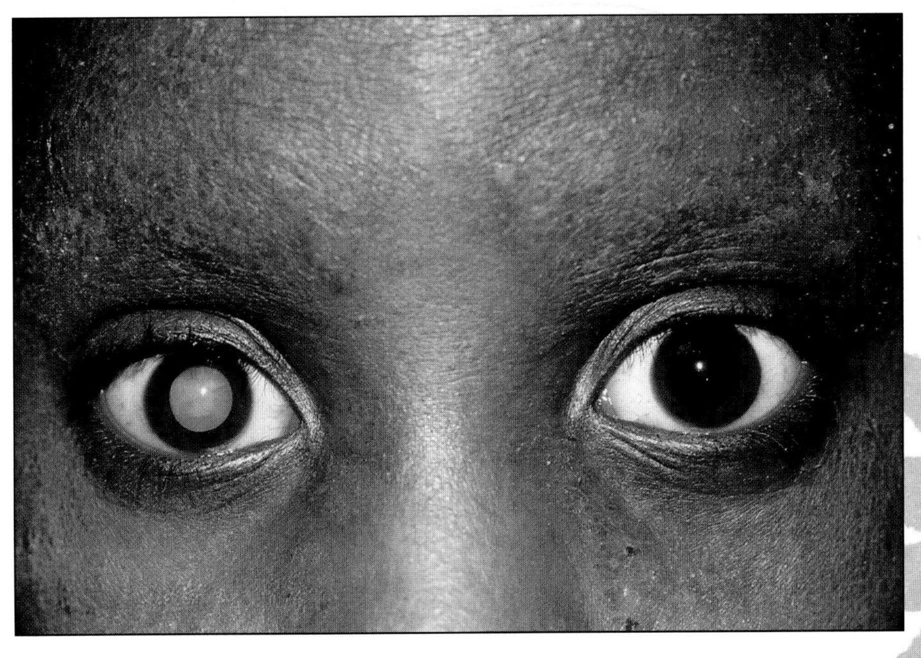

▲ Millions of people throughout the world are blind. In poor countries, blindness is often caused by infectious diseases. Blindness can also occur if people develop cataracts, which means that the lens of one or both eyes becomes cloudy. If someone has cataracts, their lenses can easily be removed by an operation, and then the patient has to wear strong glasses to replace his or her own lenses.

Never look directly at the sun because your lens focuses the light onto the retina at the back of your eye. This may destroy part of your retina, and it may never fully recover.

SPLITTING LIGHT

White light is a mixture of many colors. The range of colors that make up white light is called the spectrum. As we have already seen, all colors of light are bent when they pass from one transparent material to another. However, some colors of light are bent more than others. Violet light is bent the most and red light is bent the least.

In the seventeenth century English scientist, Sir Isaac Newton, used a triangular prism of glass to bend and split light. You can do this with a mirror and water as shown here. ▶

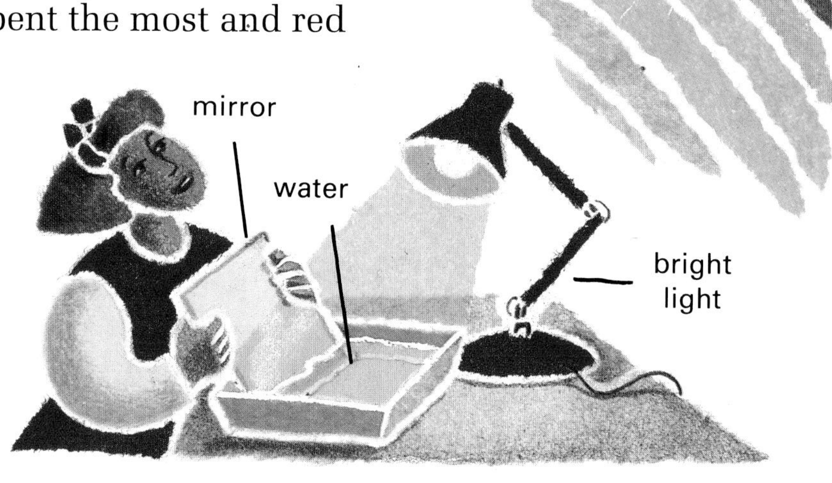

◀ Drops of water can also split light and form rainbows in the air. You can see these in the spray from a lawn sprinkler on a sunny day. The great arch of a rainbow is made by the light falling on drops of water hanging in the air shortly after a rain. Many different legends have been told about rainbows. One tale was that rainbows were bridges between the earth and heaven. Other stories told about the great riches hidden at the ends of rainbows.

WHY IS IT RED?

Objects appear colored because they reflect some colors of light and absorb others. Some materials have special chemicals called pigments that do this. The pigment chlorophyll, which is in plant leaves, reflects only green light and absorbs all other colors. Similarly, a red object reflects red light and absorbs all other colors. White objects reflect all the colors of the spectrum, but black objects absorb all of them so that no light is reflected. ▼

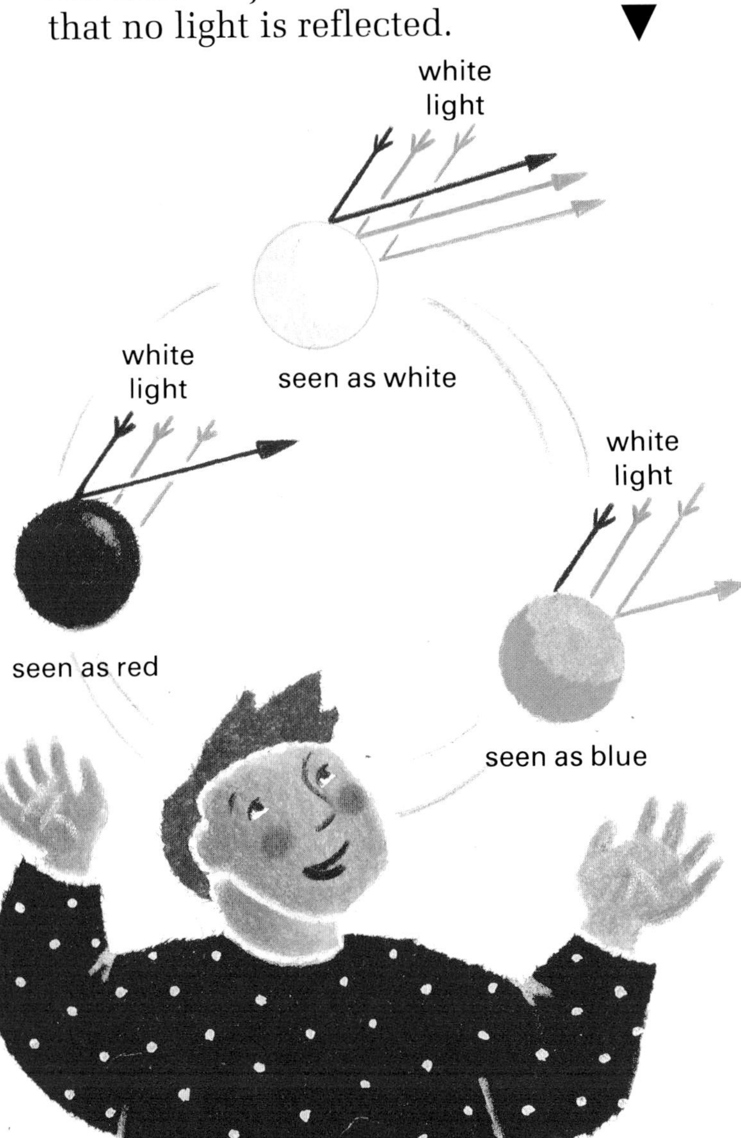

▲ Sometimes, rays of light are reflected off particles in the air in such a way that the sky turns beautiful shades of red, orange, and yellow.

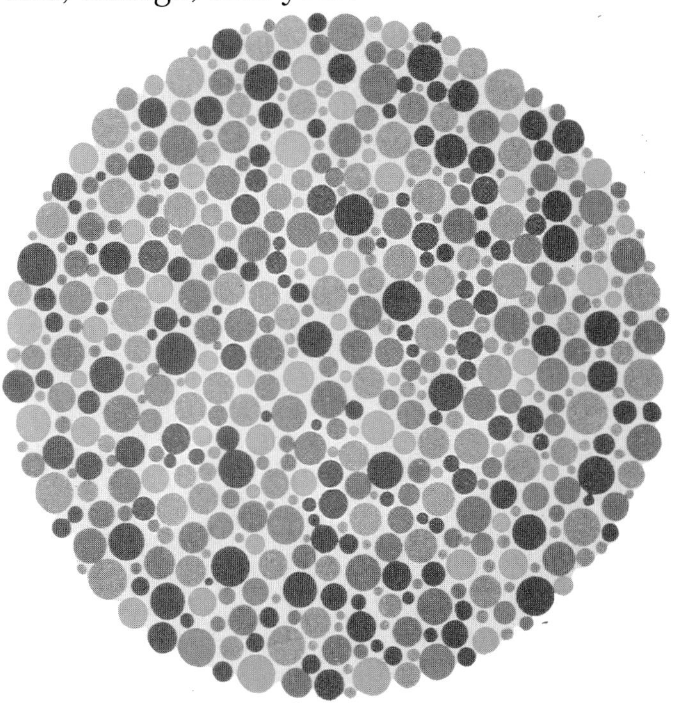

▲ There are a few people who can't see colors very well. We say they are "color blind." People who are color blind usually find it difficult to see the difference between shades of red and green. There are a number of tests designed to check for color blindness. People with red and green color blindness wouldn't be able to see a number in this circle.

MIXING COLORED LIGHT

If you mix different colors of light together, you don't get the same results as when you mix paints together. For example, mix all the colors in your paint box together and you'll probably end up with a dark brown. But if you mix all the colors of the spectrum, you make white light.

Making Secondary Colors

Red, green, and blue are the primary colors of light. All the colors of the spectrum can be made by mixing these three primary colors together. When only two primary colors are mixed they produce secondary colors. You can try making secondary colors yourself like this:

1. Cut out a circle from stiff white cardboard.
2. Divide it into six equal parts and color them in with two primary colored pens or crayons like this.
3. Make two holes $3\,^1/_2$ inches apart at the middle of the disk and loop about $1\,^1/_2$ feet of string through them.*
4. Tie the ends of the string together.
5. Spin the circle by pulling the string and slackening it when it has unwound.

*If you don't have any string, try pushing a pencil through the middle of the circle.

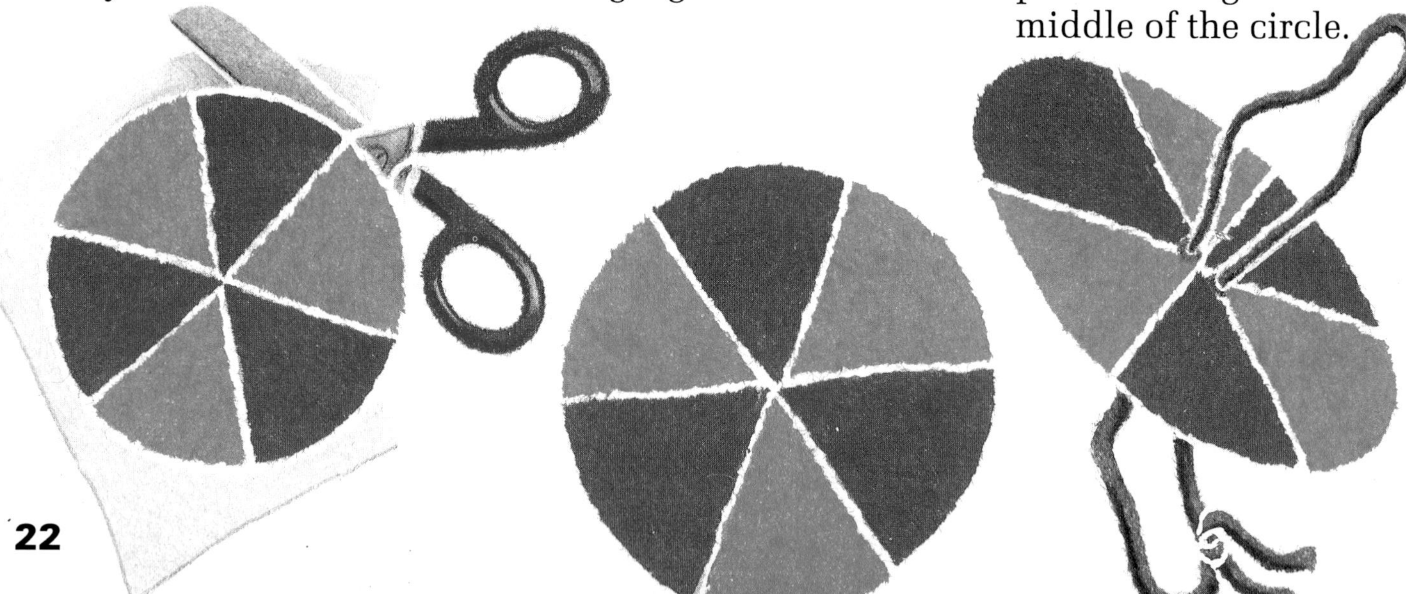

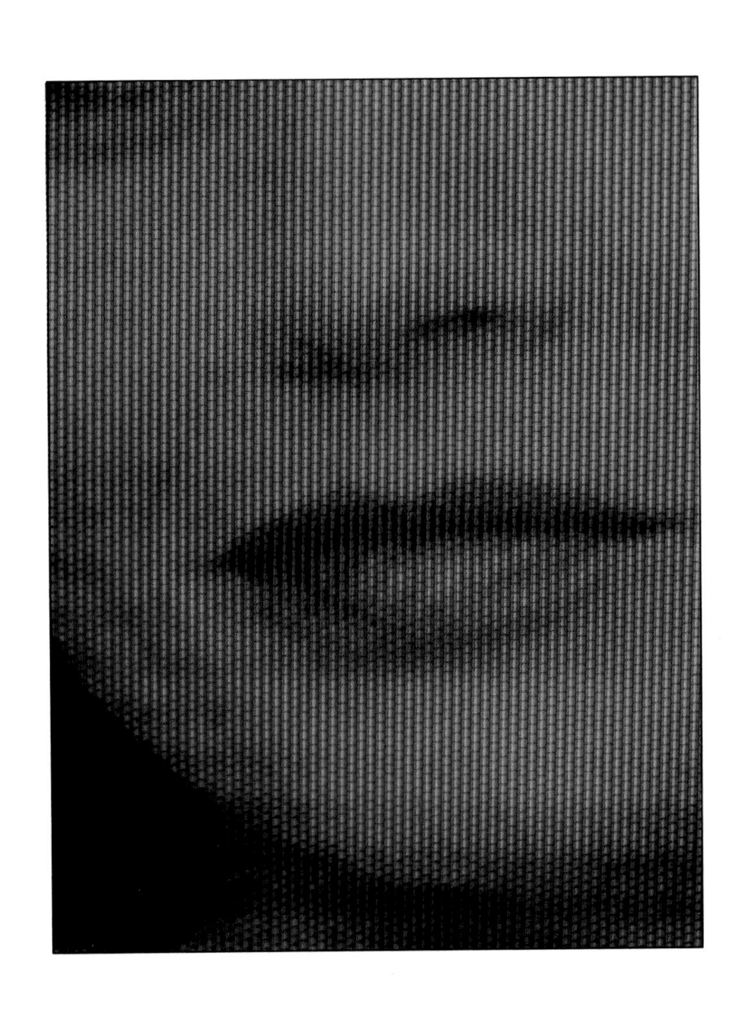

◀Color televisions work by mixing the primary colors of light together. In fact, if you look very closely at the screen you can see spots of red, green, and blue. At normal viewing distance, these spots merge together so we see a sharp color picture.

Colored substances like ink are mixtures of different pigments. These can be split up by using a process called chromatography. When ink is soaked up by absorbent paper, each different pigment moves a different distance. This separates the different pigments. Black ink is best to use for this activity because it contains a large number of different pigments.

Try experimenting with the different pairs of primary colors. You should get the following results:

red + green = yellow
blue + red = magenta
blue + green = cyan

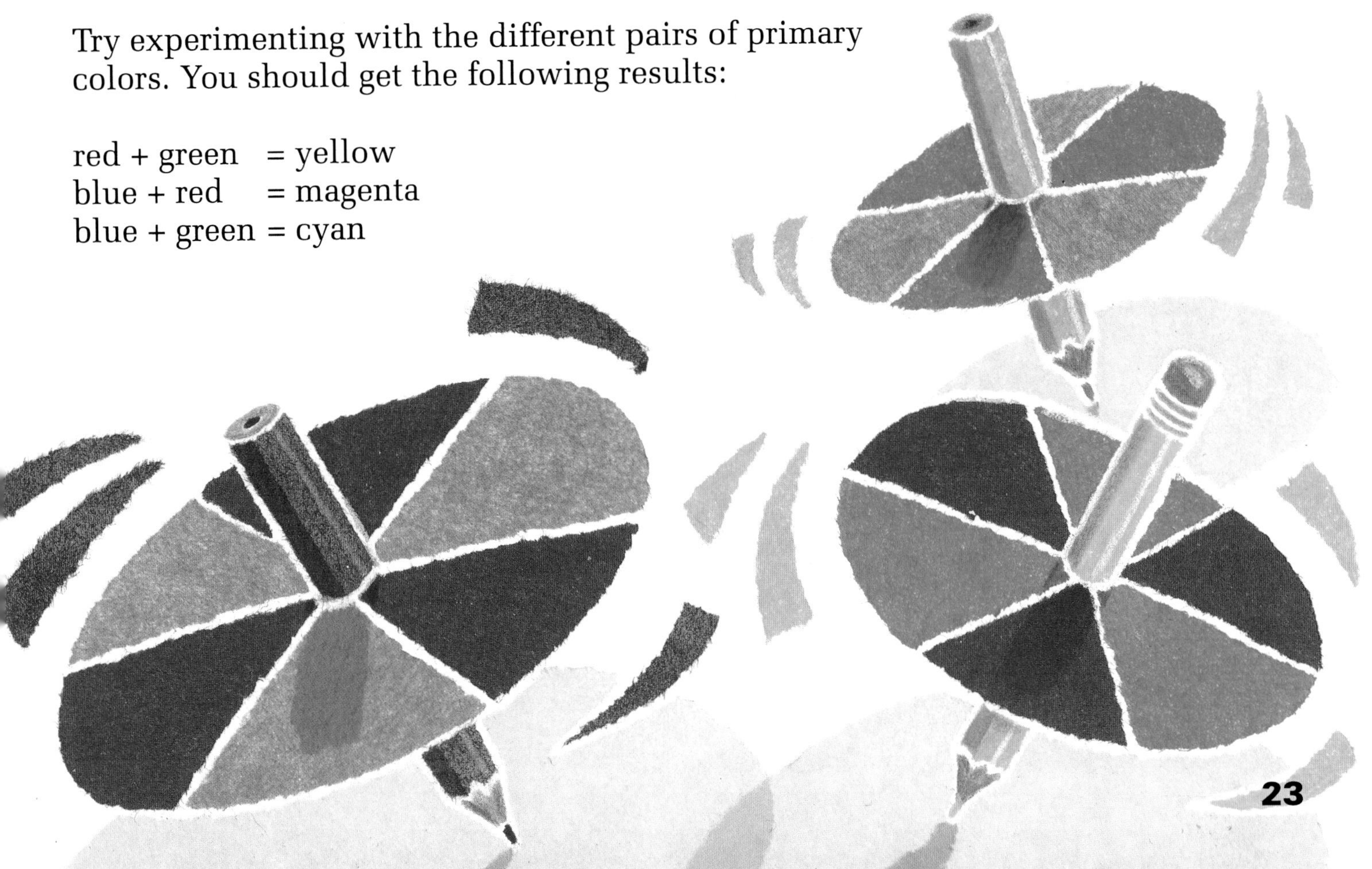

ANIMAL SIGHT AND LIGHT

Most animals have some type of eyes. Even very simple creatures like earthworms have light-sensitive patches on their skin so that they can avoid bright, sunny places where they are easy prey for birds. Larger animals, such as rabbits, are hunted and need all-around vision to spot predators like foxes. Their eyes are on the sides of their heads. Predators have forward-facing eyes so that they can judge distances better when they move in to kill their prey.

You can see how much you need two ▶ eyes if you close one eye and try to touch the end of someone else's finger.

◀ Fish have eyes that are adapted to seeing underwater. The archerfish of Central America needs to see insects resting on leaves above the water. To allow it to do this, its eyes are divided into two parts, one to look above the water and the other to look below. When it spots an insect sitting overhead, it squirts up a jet of water that knocks the insect into the river where it is quickly gobbled up!

WOW!
Giant squids have the biggest eyes in the animal kingdom. Their eyes are as big as dinner plates.

◀ Some animals use color to attract mates. The male peacock's huge colored tail shows females what a healthy mate he would make. Other animals use color to warn off possible attackers. Yellow and black stripes tell other animals that bees and wasps can sting powerfully. Diamond markings show that the rattlesnake should be avoided by larger animals looking for an easy dinner. ▼

Light from the sun never reaches some of the deepest parts of the sea. However, it is not completely dark, because many of the fish that live there have luminous parts to their bodies. The deep-sea anglerfish has a long spine that hangs in front of its mouth. On the end of its spine is a glowing green bulb. Small fish that are attracted to this light end up inside the angler's huge mouth. ▶

INVISIBLE ENERGY

There are some kinds of light that you can't see, such as infrared radiation and ultraviolet light. You can feel the infrared radiation that is given out by very hot objects, such as space heaters, and you can be burned by ultraviolet light.

When pale-skinned people are exposed to ultraviolet light, their skin gets darker to protect them from this harmful radiation. Most of the ultraviolet radiation produced by the sun is absorbed in the atmosphere by a gas called ozone. Scientists are becoming increasingly concerned that the amount of ozone in the atmosphere is being reduced by some types of polluting chemicals. This means that more ultraviolet light is getting through to us on the ground. It is very important to wear a good sun block to protect your skin from ultraviolet radiation when you are outside on a sunny day.

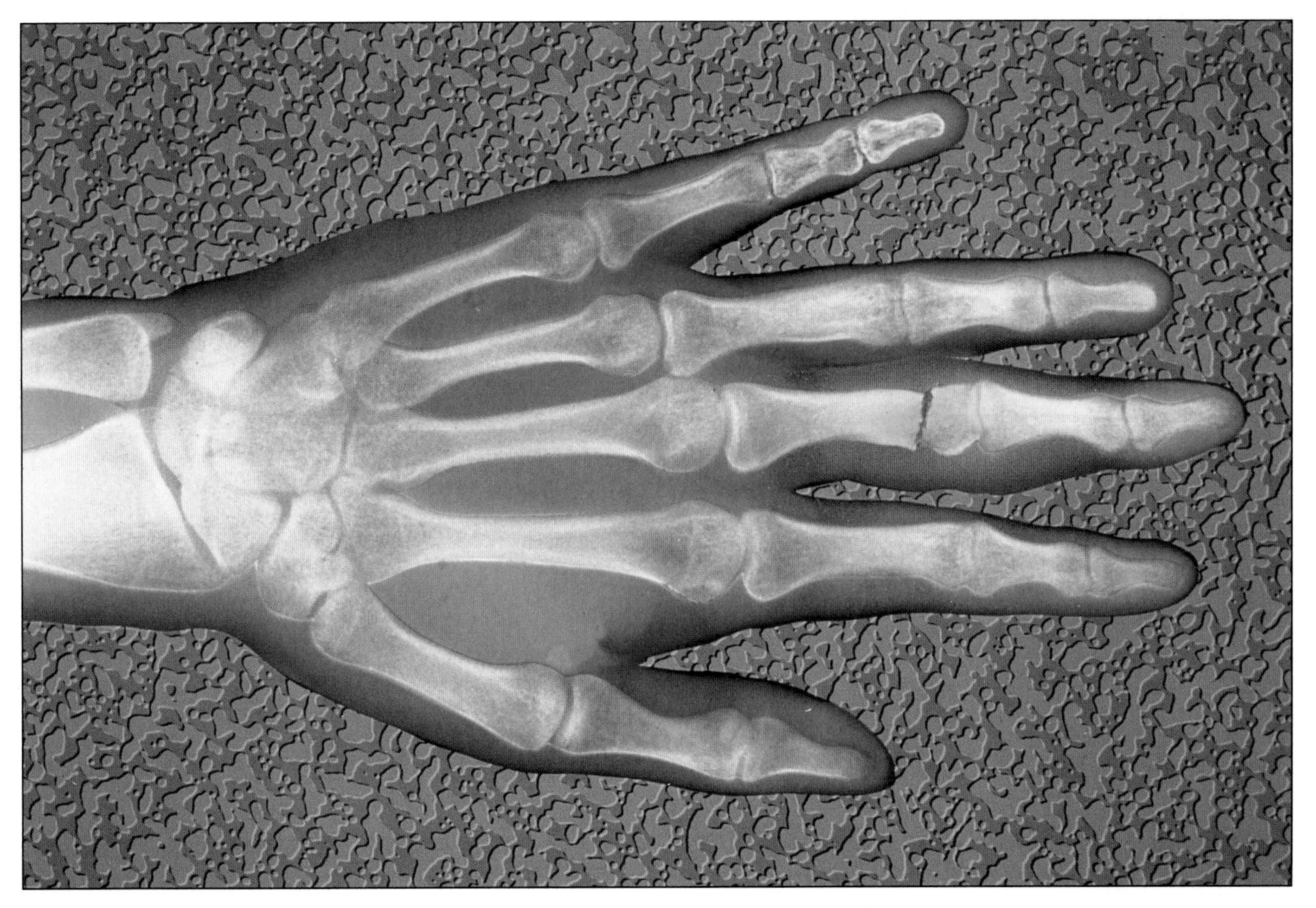

▲ X rays are a form of radiation that is very helpful in hospitals because it can travel through skin and muscle but less easily through bones. Doctors can use X rays to check for broken bones and other medical problems.

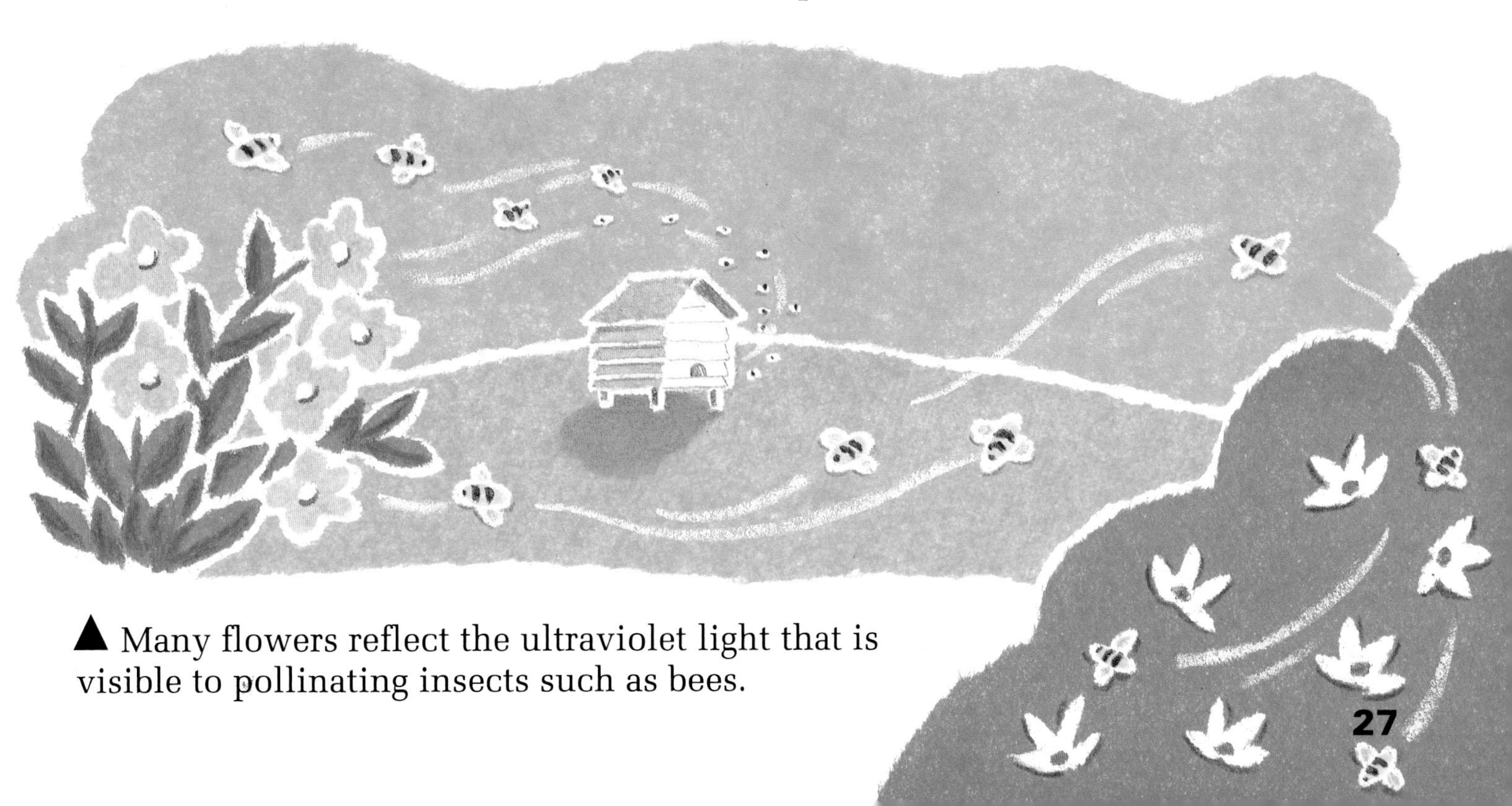

▲ Many flowers reflect the ultraviolet light that is visible to pollinating insects such as bees.

LASERS

An ordinary beam of light is a mixture of rays with different wavelengths, moving in many directions. Lasers are machines that organize light. They concentrate the rays in one direction, so that the waves of light are all in step and don't interfere with one another. This is why lasers give out a very narrow beam of light.

This is the beam of light from a laser.

This is the beam of light from a flashlight.

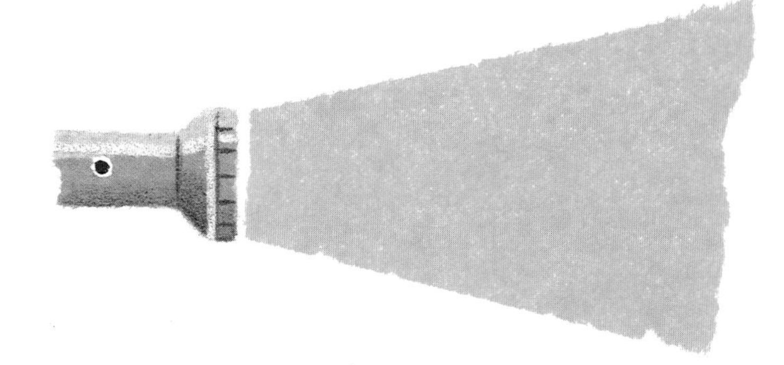

Lasers are part of everyday life. In many stores, lasers read bar code labels that carry information–like the one on the back of this book. Compact discs are played with laser beams. Doctors use laser beams to carry out delicate operations in places where cuts with a knife would cause too much bleeding. The heat from a laser beam can also seal wounds.

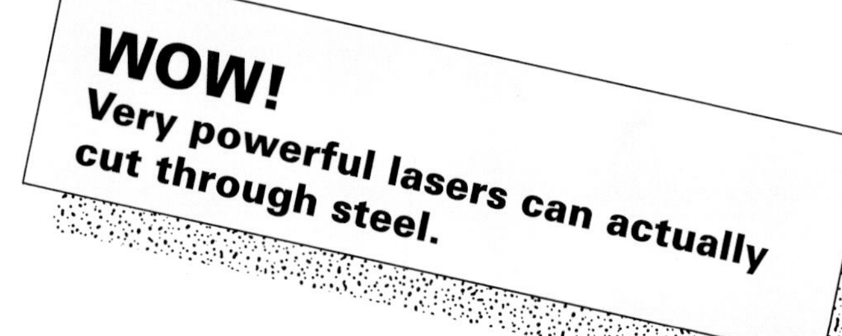

OPTIC FIBERS

▲Optic fibers are thin threads of glass or clear plastic that act like pipes for light.

Inside the fiber the beam of light is reflected off the join between the two layers of glass or plastic so that it cannot escape.

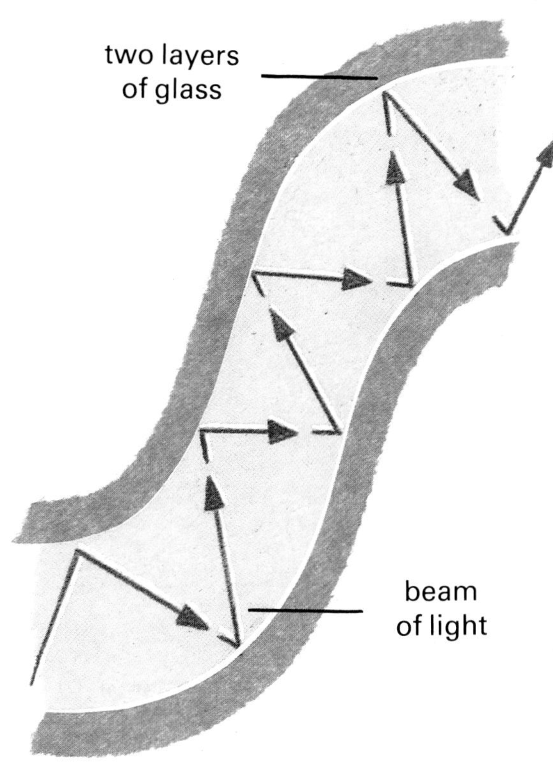

Lasers are used to send telephone messages along optic fibers. They can carry more information and are cheaper to make than the copper wires that are used to carry electrical signals for telephones.

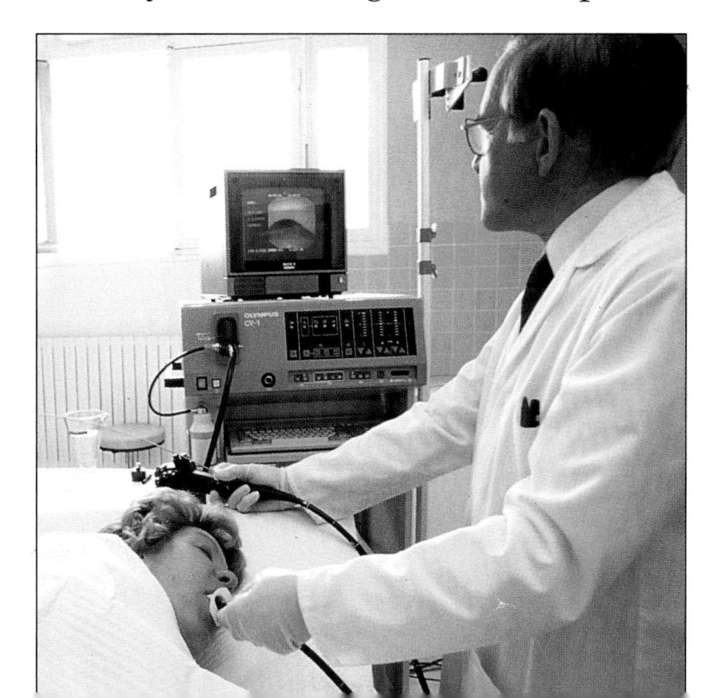

◀Doctors shine normal light through optic fibers when they want to look inside a patient's body. Light is shone down one set of optic fibers and the reflected light travels back up another set. Optic fibers allow doctors to look inside someone's stomach, or even at a baby inside its mother, without having to operate.

GLOSSARY

Astronomer A scientist who studies the stars and planets.

Chlorophyll The green pigment in plant leaves.

Concave Curving inward.

Constellations Stars that appear close to each other when viewed from earth. They may, in fact, be billions of miles apart.

Convex Curving outward.

Filament A very thin wire that gets hot when electricity passes along it.

Focus The point at which rays meet after they have been reflected. An image looks clear when it is in focus.

Glucose A simple type of sugar.

Laser A device that sends a powerful narrow beam of light.

Luminous A luminous object reflects light. It glows.

Opaque Blocking light from passing through.

Optic fiber A transparent fiber that acts like a pipe down which light can travel.

Optic nerve The connection between the retina and the brain.

Phosphor A chemical that glows when struck by electrons.

Photosynthesis The process by which plants make sugar from carbon dioxide, water, and the energy from the sun.

Pigment Colored materials that reflect their own color but absorb all the others.

Primary colors Red, green, and blue are the primary colors of light that can produce all the other colors in the spectrum when mixed together.

Secondary colors Magenta, yellow, and cyan, which are each produced by mixing two of the primary colors of light.

Solar cell A device that makes electricity directly from light.

Star A ball of glowing gas.

Telescope An instrument that focuses and magnifies the light from distant objects.

Translucent Allowing only some light to pass through.

Transparent Allowing light to pass through it almost as if the material wasn't there.

Turbine A device that has blades like a propeller, which turn to drive a generator that makes electricity.

Ultraviolet The type of light that causes people's skin to darken.

X rays A powerful type of light that can pass through skin.

BOOKS TO READ

There are lots of topics in this book for you to explore further. Here are just a few suggestions for books to read to get you started:

Asimov, Isaac. *How Did We Find Out About the Speed of Light?* New York: Walker, 1986.

Craig, Annabel and Cliff Rosney. *The Usborne Science Encyclopedia.* Tulsa: EDC, 1989.

Friedhoffer, Robert. *Light.* Scientific Magic; Book 5. New York: Franklin Watts, 1992.

Peacock, Graham. *Light.* Science Activities. New York: Thomson Learning, 1993.

Simon, Hilda. *The Magic of Color.* New York: Lothrop, Lee & Shepard, 1981.

Taylor, Barbara. *Light.* Focus On. New York: Gloucester, 1992.

Ward, Alan. *Light and Color.* Project Science. New York: Franklin Watts, 1992.

Watson, Philip. *Light Fantastic.* New York: Lothrop, Lee & Shepard, 1983.

INDEX